Good Things

FOR A YOUNG WOMAN'S SPIRIT

by Chiquis Barrón
Illustrated by Martha Barrón

GOOD THINGS FOR A YOUNG WOMAN'S SPIRIT Copyright © 2015 by Chiquis Barrón

All rights reserved. No part of this publication may be reproduced, stored in a retrieval system or transmitted in any form or by any means, electronic, mechanical, photocopying, recording or otherwise, without the written permission of the publisher, except in the case of brief quotations embodied in critical articles and reviews.

Certain trademarks are used under license.

Printed in the United States of America.

Azul Celeste Arts, LLC
9037 N. Palm Brook Drive
Tucson, AZ 85743
www.chiquisbarron.com

Second Edition, April 2019

ISBN 978-0-9970435-2-5

For Ana Fernanda & Isabella María

Introduction

Art and literature have always been an important source of social catharsis. They allow creators a means for release and self-expression, while also affording the audience who experience the resulting creative pieces an opportunity to find meaning and healing in the context of their own lives. *Good Things for a Young Woman's Spirit* is a collection of soul-nourishing messages and illustrations to help young women understand that they are not alone in their feelings and experiences. No matter how difficult or dark life may sometimes seem, these empowering words and artwork will permeate through to infuse their spirit with hope, knowledge, and the promise of bright, colorful days ahead.

Reach for the Stars

Believe. Trust in yourself and in your capacity to do the things you aspire to no matter how far-fetched or improbable they may seem. Naysayers come a dime a dozen. Don't let them drain you of your confidence and enthusiasm. Reach for the stars fearlessly. Take a deep breath and extend your arms high with determination. The sky is yours.

Share Your Talents Selflessly

Being noticed and standing out in a crowd is a wonderful experience, but there is also beauty in knowing how to humbly allow your greatness to subtly shine. You are gifted and have many contributions to offer the world. Share your talents selflessly even if you don't receive public recognition or acknowledgement. The most rewarding feelings of accomplishment, satisfaction, and joy often come from quiet self-validation.

Practice Kindness

Practice kindness toward yourself and others. Nothing defuses feelings of insecurity, inadequacy, or anger more effectively than genuine compassion. It is easy to fall into the alluring habit of malicious gossip and trash-talk, particularly when it comes to people you feel have mistreated or offended you. The sense of pleasure it produces, however, is fleeting and mediocre at best and quickly leaves you feeling miserable once again. Show people kindness instead—in thought, word, and action—and you'll be surprised to witness the wonders it creates both in their spirit and yours.

Enjoy Your Present Moment

Stay informed on current events but don't get caught up in the sensationalist spiral. There are hundreds of tragedies that take place around the world daily. Be aware of them and send an earnest wish for solace, hope, and healing, but don't let them keep you from relishing the immediate joys and beauty in your life. Practice kindness actively each day for the ripples created with each small act can have far-reaching global effects.

Radiate Positivity

Be especially kind with people who revel in other's misfortunes. It is amazing how a little compassion can help rewire the inner workings of a broken or bruised spirit. Be the generous force that helps trigger small yet far-reaching bursts of positive, bright energy into the world.

Forgive Freely

Forgiveness is one of the most cathartic gifts we can give to ourselves. Letting go of vengeful, negative feelings and attitudes provides the perfect relief—both mental and physical—so that we may renew, restore, and move onward and upward. Be quick to forgive others, but be just as quick and willing to forgive yourself.

Cultivate Real Friendships

There have always been people who enjoy collecting "friends". They seldom establish any deep, meaningful, or long-lasting bonds with anyone but find a deluded sense of validation and worth by surrounding themselves with lots of people. The invention of social media has provided the perfect platform for these kinds of collectors to attract and amass virtual friends even when no real or solid connections exist.

As you delve into the wonders of modern-day technology and carefully strategize ways to increase friend and follower numbers, make sure you don't forsake your good, old-fashioned, flesh-and-bone friends. Although they may be few, there is no virtual number that amounts to the extraordinary quality and substance these friends possess.

Experience Your Feelings Fully

Don't be afraid to feel. Experiencing emotion, both good and bad, is one of the most basic human functions. Don't let a culture of desensitization, where emotional expression is often considered a weakness, rob you of that wonderful experience that is intrinsically a part of you.

Let Go

Practice the art of letting go. We often cling to people, traditions, situations, and material things even though we know deep down that they are not really what we want, what makes us happy, nor what is good for us. As we loosen our grip on those ill-fitting aspects of our lives, we open ourselves for the opportunity to receive the things that truly complement us and suit us well. Harness your strength to let go.

Ease Into Change

Change, even desired change, can be quite daunting. It requires that we let go of that which has been a part of us and prepare to receive the unknown. Open your arms wide to release the old and then embrace the new and unfamiliar with utmost grace and finesse. Be grateful for periods of restlessness and adjustment because it means you are morphing into your next phase—that is what growth is. Take the time to adapt; allow yourself to feel the awkwardness of the transition. It's an important and necessary step in the process and acting on impulse to speed it up is a shortcut that never pans out. Take a deep breath. Unfold with ease into the beauty of your new form. You are safe. It is only change.

Find Your Own Truth

One of the most important realizations we can make is understanding that life is too complex to label things simply as right or wrong, true or false. What is right and true for some may be equally wrong and false for others. Focus instead on finding the rightness and truth that most wholly nourish your life and most fully bring peace and happiness to your spirit.

Be Flexible and Fluid

Always feel free to change your mind. Life is a journey full of trial and error. Decisions you make early on as you embark on your journey do not have to bind nor dictate who you will be or what you must do the rest of your life. We are evolving beings with an incredible ability to learn from our experiences and missteps, to adapt and to grow. Embrace both your successes and mistakes and allow them to shape you into the strong, wise and confident person you are meant to become.

Explore the World

Travel. Move around. Wander unfamiliar grounds. Nothing gives us a better perspective or more effectively teaches us what is truly valuable than experiencing life outside of our comfortable little bubbles. Things that once seemed infinitely gorgeous or catastrophic in our small worlds will seem minuscule when compared to the vast beauty and tragedy that exists beyond our known boundaries. Transcend them. Explore freely.

Embrace Solitude

Living deeply often requires that we sit quietly with ourselves and our thoughts. Practice finding the beauty and confidence that come from being on your own without the need to buffer natural self-doubts and insecurities with unnecessary and oftentimes unhealthy company. You have the ability to work through any personal uncertainty or anxiety if you just allow the time to be with yourself. Embrace your solitude and you will soon find that your own presence is enough. Everyone and everything else is only the icing on the cake.

Take a Step Back

Finishing first and in front is wonderful. However, don't be afraid to take a few steps back. Oftentimes, we can only appreciate the beautiful colors and scenery of a panoramic view when we position ourselves behind others. Many of the most meaningful details that make our experiences whole and profound require that wide-angle perspective.

See Beyond the Sparkle

Take the time to truly see the people and the world around you, even when they don't shine brightly at first glance. Celebrities and media personalities have a glow and charm that's very alluring. However, give yourself the opportunity to look away from the hypnotizing glare to find the often much more radiant, albeit subtle, sparkle in those doing wonders in anonymity.

Always Choose You

Make yourself your number one choice. When it comes to choosing between being loyal to yourself—your values, your beliefs, your happiness, your success, your health and your overall well-being—or being true to someone who will only accept you if you change essential bits and pieces of who you are, always choose yourself. You are whole, brilliant and complete just as you are.

Grow from Loss

Among the myriad of emotions we experience in our lives, perhaps the most dreaded yet necessary of all is a sense of loss. Whether it is the loss of someone or something we hold dear, there is no shortcut past the pain. Despite the agony, however, peace eventually draws us closer and solace slowly begins to seep in, soothing the tender soul with every breath.

When you are faced with loss, surround yourself with those whose presence brings you joy, however subtle it may be. Soon the sadness will begin to dissipate and your thoughts will turn to the vast beauty of surviving memories. If you continue to love and pray and live fully, happiness will trickle in once again and, one day, at the end of the unabridged journey, you'll realize how much resiliency and internal strength your soul has gained.

Welcome Knowledge

Never, ever stop learning. You have the ability to absorb a limitless amount of knowledge. No matter how old or experienced you become, always remain open to new information and different points of view. As philosopher George Santayana said, "The wisest mind has something yet to learn."

Laugh at Yourself

Don't take yourself too seriously. In the end, we are all human. We make mistakes and inevitably goof up. If you're lucky, you'll goof up quite a bit and each time will present a new opportunity for growth and learning. Learn to laugh at yourself. There are few things more nourishing and liberating for the soul than laughter.

Trust Your Instincts

One of the most paralyzing feelings in life is a sense of guilt. Although feeling remorse or deep regret when we have wronged someone is natural and, in fact, healthy, beware of people who attempt to assert their power by using guilt—oftentimes unearned—as their most resourceful tool. People who cannot rationally explain why they expect certain behaviors from others will often resort to senseless guilt trips in order to continue manipulating people and situations. Do not fall into that trap. No matter how close you are to someone or how much you admire them, always allow yourself the opportunity to take a few steps back and evaluate your needs, views, and opinions independently. Listen to your heart and trust your instincts; they are your most reliable compass.

Do What's Right for You

Be courageous enough to think independently and be different. Your definitions of happiness and success are your own, others cannot define them for you; only you know what's closest to your heart.

Be Kind to Yourself

Be kind to yourself—your mind, your body, and your spirit. Caring for yourself is the best example you can set for others about being generous and charitable. When you tend to yourself and make sure you are well, you are better equipped to help others find wellness too.

Fashion Life to Your Own Style

Always be proud of the life you choose to live. Whatever path you embark on—traditional or not—make certain it is exactly what you want and what makes you happy. Do not let short-lived fads or long-standing conventions pressure you into a life that does not suit you. Fashion your life to your own style and liking and you will own the runway.

Believe in Your Worth

Hold firmly to your sense of self-worth. You may not always receive the kind of treatment and attention you deserve from others, but that, in no way, depreciates your value. Be forgiving of others' inability to appreciate your worth. Their lack of sight and awareness is their handicap and not a reflection of you. You are invaluable and worthy of all the love, joy and beauty in the world. Grasp onto it with gusto.

Take Risks

Life will not always be fair. You should give every opportunity your very best anyway. Taking risks is our heart's way of practicing courage. In the end, you may not hold all the medals but your life will be more meaningful and easier to contend with because your soul will be flexing some brave and bold muscles.

Remain True to Who You Are

People have a chameleon-like ability to adapt to new situations and around different people. It is an innate survival mechanism. One of the most liberating lessons that come with maturity is realizing that, although we can modify and alter certain aspects of ourselves to appease tense circumstances, we must not sacrifice integral parts of who we are for the purpose of easing other's insecurities and discomfort. Do not make yourself small only to indulge other's grandiose delusions.

Cherish Every Moment in Life

Life is constantly evolving. It is natural to feel a little embarrassed when looking at old pictures or personal memorabilia. Move through those feelings with grace but do not destroy the evidence. Every phase we live through has its worth and serves as a reference point for where we've been and where we're heading. Soon nostalgia and appreciation will replace all other emotions. Wait for them. Savor them.

Never Give Up

Nothing strengthens your soul or forges your character like failing at something and finding the heart to go at it again. Disappointment and rejection are an inevitable and necessary part of life, but they don't have to dim your inner light permanently. When temporary setbacks occur, pick yourself up gently and take the next step in the direction of your dreams with intention. Persevere. A bright and bountiful future awaits you.

About the Author & the Illustrator

Chiquis Barrón is a behavioral and medical researcher with the University of Arizona. Her work in academia is closely tied to and inspires many of the themes in her creative projects. Chiquis is also author of the International Latino Book Award-winning novel *Café Dulcet* and creator and editor of Art Motif Magazine. She currently resides in Tucson, AZ.

Martha Barrón is a lifelong recreational artist and crafter. She currently lives in Nogales, AZ with her husband of 48 years and their 11-year old Shih Tzu, Petunia.

www.ingramcontent.com/pod-product-compliance
Lightning Source LLC
Chambersburg PA
CBHW041441010526
44118CB00003B/145